BACH FOR EARLY GRADES

BOOK I

Compiled from

ANNA MAGDALENE'S NOTE-BOOK

By

Bryceson Treharne

Biographical Sketch
By
Laurence B. Ellert

THE BOSTON MUSIC COMPANY

DISTRIBUTED BY

HAL•LEONARD® CORPORATION

7777 W. BLUEMOUND RD. P.O. BOX 13819 MILWAUKEE, WI 53213

B. M. Co. 9584

Bach playing for Frederick the Great

"THERE is only one Bach", exclaimed Frederick the Great when he heard that master of oratorio, JOHANN SEBASTIAN BACH, improvise on his pianofortes and organs at the palace in Potsdam.

Born in Eisenach, a Thuringian village in Germany, March 21, 1685, little Sebastian's family was known throughout the country as one of musicians. Between 1500 and 1871, fifty-two descendants covered the four generations. His great-great grandfather, Veit Bach, a jovial miller, strummed his instrument and sang lustily while the noisy mill-wheel was grinding his grain. Sebastian's father, Johann Ambrosius Bach, a viola player and organist in the village church, gave him lessons on the violin and encouraged him to become a great musician. When the lad was nine years old his mother died; the following year he lost his father. So his eldest brother, Johann Christoph, fourteen years older and a very fine musician, took charge of the orphans. He lived in Ohrduff, a village thirty miles from Eisenach, and here the children were sent to school at the *Gymnasium* to study literature, religion and—of course—music. It was difficult to get music in those days and Christoph, who had quite a library which he kept under lock and key, refused to let the boy have some sheets he wished to copy. Sebastian found a way to gain access to the bookcase, and night after night, for six months, copied them by moonlight. At the age of fourteen, he set out from home with another boy to walk to Lüneburg, a village 200 miles away, where they applied as choir boys at St. Michael's. Bach's facility for reading music and his lovely voice so engaged the singing master that he was urged to remain. Besides developing a knowledge of church music he heard the distinguished organist Böhm. Soon he began to "walk over to Hamburg", a distance of thirty miles to hear the great organ master, Reinken, of St. Katherine's, give concerts. A story is told that he sat down to rest on a bench outside an inn, undoubtedly wishing he had the money to enter and partake of some of the delicious sausage, the cooking aroma of which tempted his appetit . Someone must have seen him, for suddenly, two herring heads were thrown out the window. Sebastian picked them up, and inside each mouth found a gold piece. After satisfying his hunger, he undoubtedly returned to Hamburg to hear more music

In 1703 he secured a position as organist in a new church at Arnstadt where his salary, including allowance for board and lodging, was about $50.00 a year. Here, on a new organ, he was free to expand his love of playing and composing. He began to write those elaborate Toccatas and Fugues. At the age of twenty-two he married his little cousin Maria Barbara and received a small "dot" to set up housekeeping in Mühlhausen where he accepted a new post. The environment was not to his liking so he went to Weimar, where he had a choir of about twelve and a very substantial income. Here at the court of Saxe-Weimar he was made director of concerts and had to compose a cantata every month besides special pieces for birthdays, weddings, funerals, etc. A contest was arranged by King Ferdinand in Dresden between Bach and the celebrated Marchand, organist to Louis XV of France. On his arrival he heard Bach at practice, when it was time for the contest Marchand could not be found. At his hotel it was said that he had left Dresden by fast coach.

In 1717, Bach was engaged as Kappell-meister by Prince Leopold of Anhalt-Cöthen. So he packed up his family and moved to greater opportunities. At Cöthen he wrote the immortal "48 Preludes and Fugues". He frequently accompanied the Prince on journeys. Returning from one of the tours he learned that his wife, after a short illness, had died and was buried before he could be informed. Two of their children, Wilhelm Friedmann and Carl Philipp Emmanuel became famous musicians.

Bach Monument, Eisenach

In 1721, he married a musician, Anna Magadelena, who bore him thirteen children, managed his household, copied out his works and was the source of greatest inspiration to him for the next thirty-one years. Toward the end, his eyes began to fail and nothing could be done to prevent blindness. He died July 28, 1750.

There was always music in the Bach family, all the children studied and nothing gave Bach greater pleasure then to gather his family around him and play music.

NOTE: *This is a mere sketch—the human side—of one of the greatest figures in musical history. There are many biographies such as C. S. Terry's translation of Forkel's "Johann Sebastian Bach" which students are sure to enjoy.*

L. B. E.

Anna Magdalene's Note-Book   *Original manuscript in the Prussian State-Library at Berlin*

I N olden times, musical people wrote down their favorite pieces and kept them in neatly bound books. Three of such books were in the Bach family: *"The Clavier Book"* prepared for the eldest son, Friedemann: a book containing the first five *French Suites* and a few smaller compositions, inscribed: "For Anna Magdalene Bach", and the famous *Note-Book* (1725) as reproduced above. The original of this book has a cover of green paper, the edges of which are stamped with a gold border. The initials and date are in gold letters. The additional letters, spelling out "Anna Magdel. Bach" in ink, are in the handwriting of Philip Emanuel and were undoubtedly added later. According to the date, it seems to have been given to Anna by Sebastian on her twenty-fourth birthday.

Anna Magdalene, born Sept. 22, 1701, was the youngest daughter of a musician, Johann Casper Wülcken, who held an appointment as trumpeter to the Court at Zeitz. In 1714, he was transferred to the Duke of Weissenfels' Court and here Anna seems to have appeared in concerts. A few years later, she won fame as "Singer to the Prince" in Cöthen. Sebastian Bach, a widower since July, 1720, and the Court conductor of music, fell in love with this lovely singer of twenty and, on Dec. 3, 1721, they were married. Two years later, the couple, with the children of Bach's first marriage, moved to Leipzig.

Many interesting and charming legends have grown up around the "Note-Book". In his biography of Bach, Phillip Spitta calls it "an intimate, tender relationship between husband and wife." However, there is no reason to suppose it was ever intended as a record of Bach's own compositions. In 1725, he wrote out two of his piano suites in the book and after that, he seems to have surrendered the book entirely to the fancy of his wife's taste. A third of the pieces in the "Note-Book" are in Anna's handwriting. The contents seems to cover a long period and for months at a time, there are no entries. Meanwhile, the children were growing up and needed teaching pieces to play on the clavichord or music for dancing—*marches, gavottes, minuets, polonaises, etc.* As Papa Bach was always a busy man, it rested upon the lovable, unselfish Anna to collect simple and practical material. As the children grew up they also tried their hand at composing and Mother's beloved music-book became a convenient place to jot it down. The piety and devotion of the Bachs accounts for the frequent appearances of Chorales and religious music.

Anna Magdalene outlived her husband about ten years and died Feb. 27, 1760, destitute and dependent on charity. She lies buried in St. Joseph's Cemetery (Leipzig), beside her husband.

Chorale

Wie wohl ist mir, o Freund der Seelen
(What joy is mine, o Friend of mortals)

1

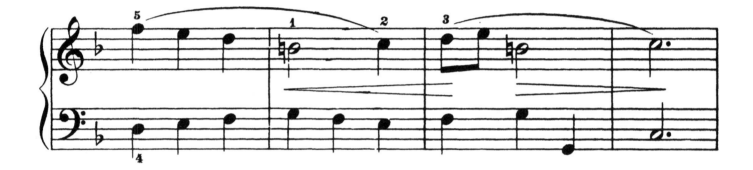

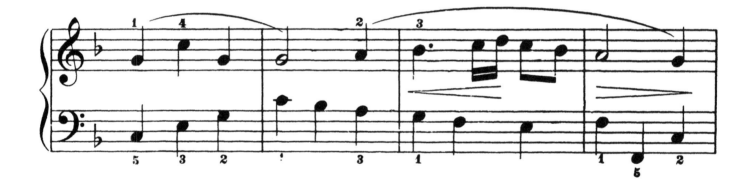

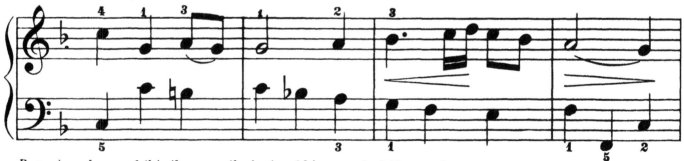

Busoni made use of this theme as the basis of his second violin sonata.

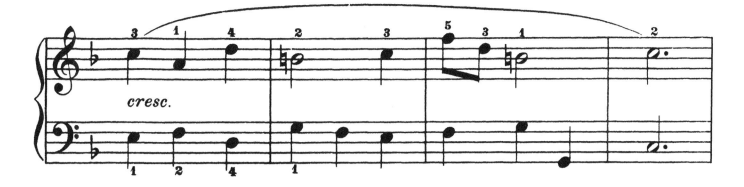

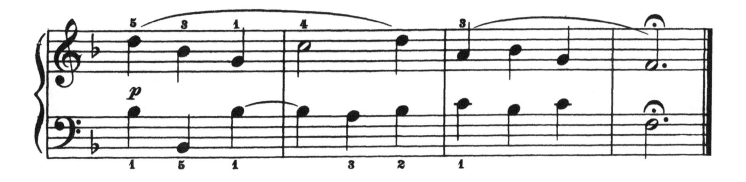

Chorale

Do as Thou will'st with me, O Lord!

A text, "Schaff's mit mir, Gott," by Benjamin Schmolck (without music) appeared in a Dresden song book dated 1725. The composer of the melody is unknown but Bach harmonized it for Anna Magdalene.

B.M.Co. 9584

Aria

When my pipe I smoke

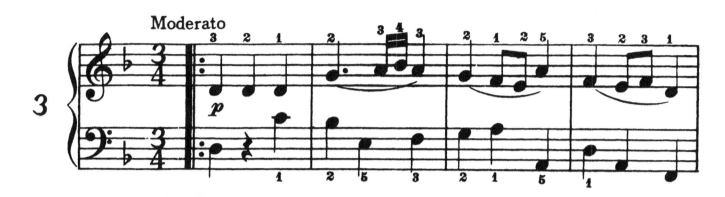

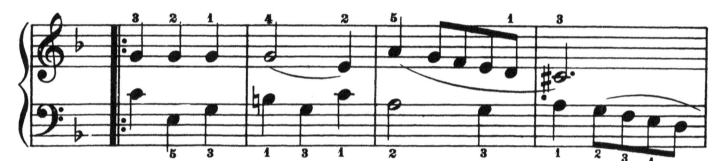

This "Aria" appears twice in the "Note-Book"; the version above in the key of D minor without words and another in G minor with words. The latter was undoubtedly transposed within the range of Anna Magdalene's voice and she evidently sang it to please her husband. A translation of the words is given below:

When in my pipe I take my pleasure,
  Filling it with tobacco new,
Smoking before the fire at leisure,
  Then I do learn a lesson true:
    I see in this, my pipe so fine,
    A likeness to this life of mine.

When I do light my pipe so neatly,
  In but a moment I do find,
That all the smoke has gone completely,
  Leaving but ashes here behind:
    So does man's body turn to clay,
    So does his glory fade away.

B.M.Co. 9584   *Text, Copyrighted 1939, by The Boston Music Co.*

Minuet in G major

(Fait par Mons. Böhm)

Georg Böhm

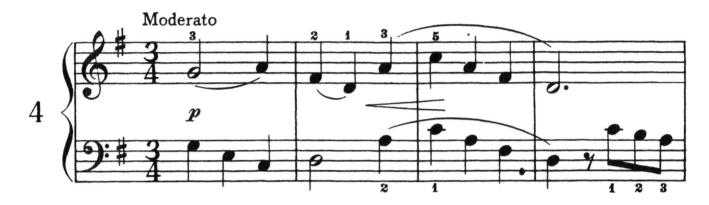

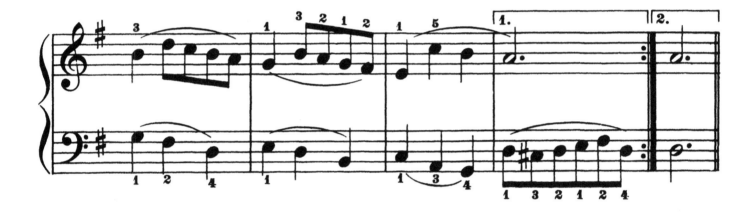

This composition was written by Georg Böhm (1661-1733) organist and former teacher of Bach in Lüneburg. The Bach's were so fond of this Minuet that it was included in the "Note-Book".

B.M.Co. 9584

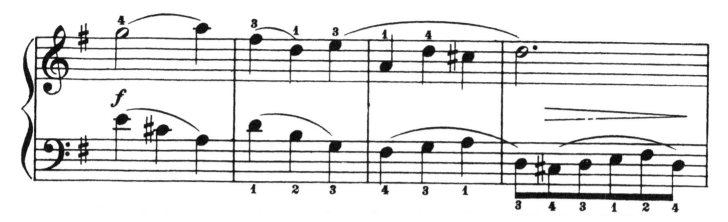

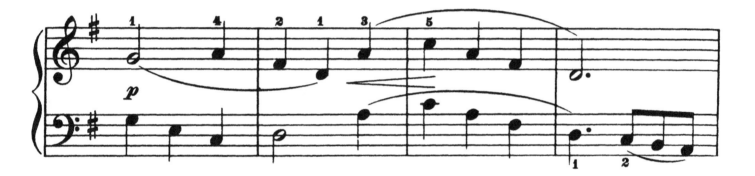

Aria

Andante

5

Chorale

O Ewigkeit, du Donnerwort!
(Oh, Eternity, thou Mighty Word!)

The text of this Chorale was written by Joh. Rist and the melody by Joh. Schop. The four-part version appears in a book of 4-pt chorals written by Bach for his son Philipp Emanuel.

B.M.Co. 9584

Minuet in G major

In the "Note-Book" this Minuet appears in the handwriting of Anna Magdalene.

B.M.Co. 9584

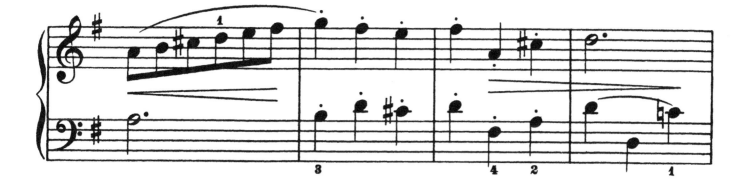

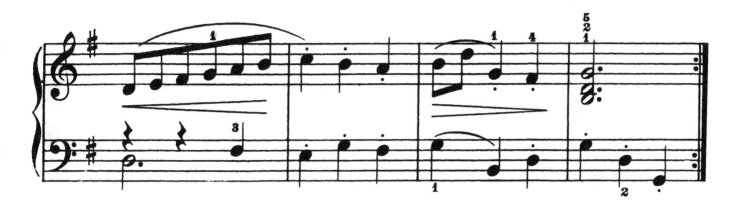

Minuet in G minor

Also in A. M.'s handwriting
B.M.Co. 9584

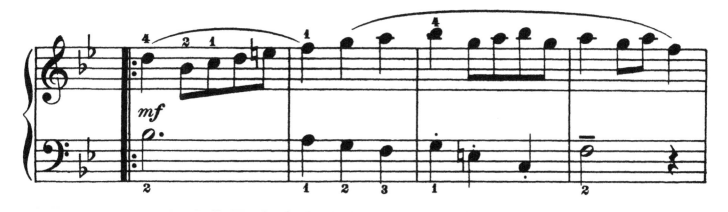

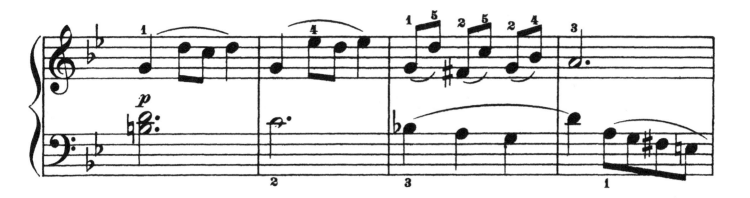

B.M.Co. 9584

Chorale

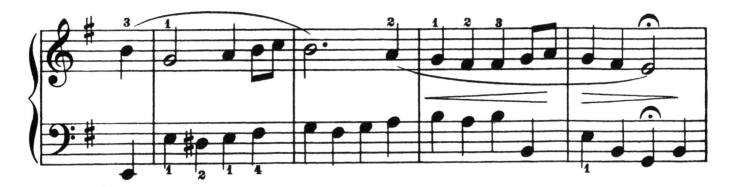

In a marginal note Philipp Emanuel wrote: "By J. S. B."

B.M.Co. 9584

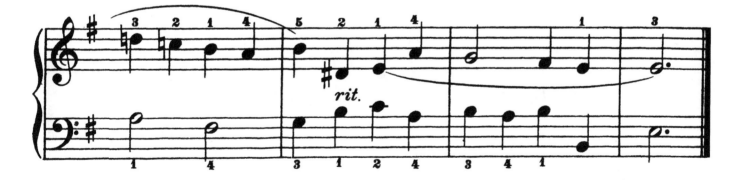

B.M.Co. 9584

Minuet in G major

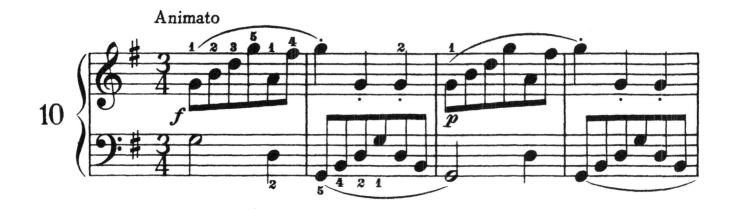

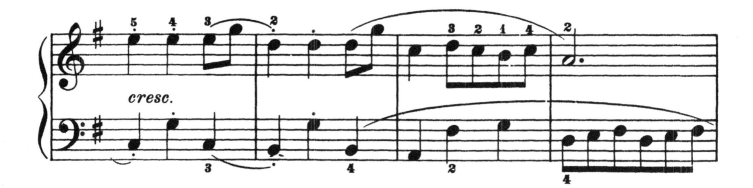

Composer unknown

B.M.Co. 9584

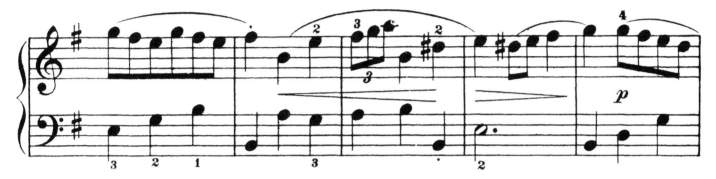

B.M.Co. 9584

March in D major

B.M.Co. 9584

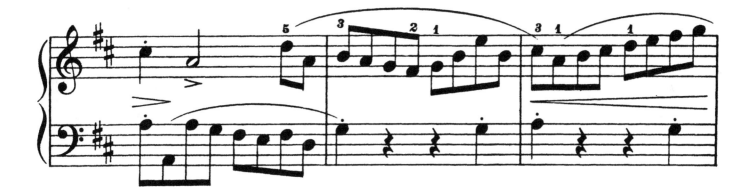

B.M.Co. 9584

Musette in D major

Allegro con brio

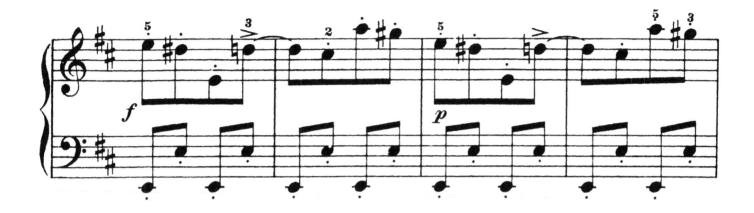

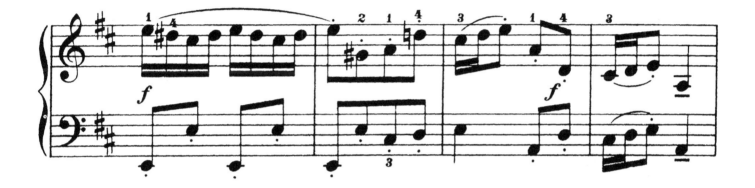

B.M.Co. 9584

Minuet in C minor

13

In A. M.'s handwriting. Composer unknown.

B.M.Co. 9584

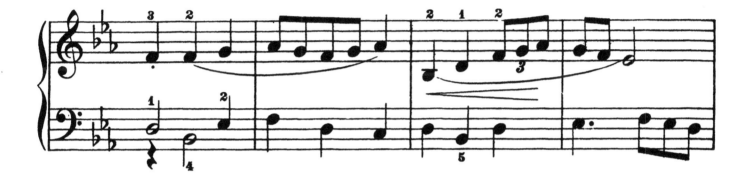

B.M.Co. 9594

Minuet in D minor

Anonymous origin. Written in an unidentified hand.

B.M.Co. 9584

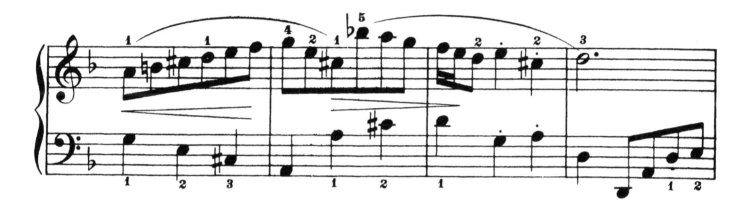

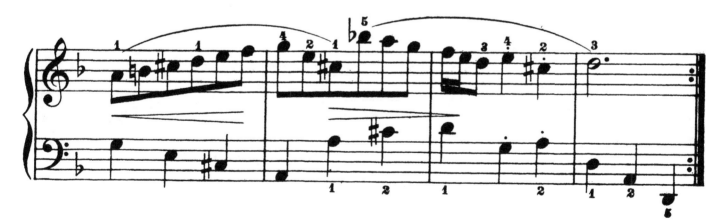

B.M.Co. 9584

March in G major

15

Anonymous origin. Written in an unidentified hand.

B.M.Co. 8584

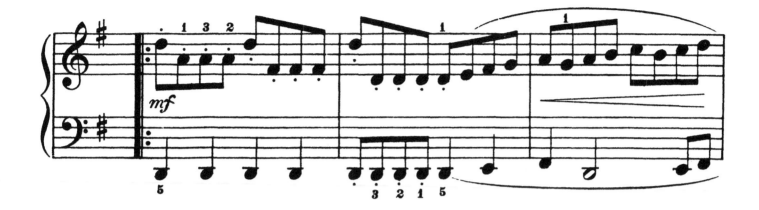

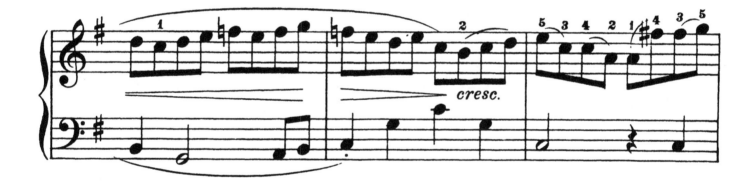

Aria di Giovannini

Polonaise in G minor